SAM CHOY'S

Little Hawaiian *Poke* Cookbook

SAM CHOY'S

Little
Hawaiian
Poke
Cookbook

Compiled by Joanne Fujita

MUTUAL PUBLISHING

This book is an abridgement of *Sam Choy's Poke – Hawai'i's Soul Food*
published in 1999

All rights reserved
ISBN 1-56647-699-2
Library of Congress Catalog Card Number: 2004112027

Design by Emily R. Lee
Photographs courtesy of Douglas Peebles.

First Printing, October 2004
Second Printing, February 2006
2 3 4 5 6 7 8 9

Mutual Publishing, LLC
1215 Center Street, Suite 210
Honolulu, Hawai'i 96816
Ph: 808-732-1709 / Fax: 808-734-4094
email: mutual@mutualpublishing.com
www.mutualpublishing.com

Printed in Korea

TABLE OF CONTENTS

Tofu and Vegetable Poke

Seviche Style

Poke with a Twist

Cooked Poke

Poke Glossary

Fish Shopping Tips

INTRODUCTION

These days, poke is everywhere in the Islands. It's on the menu in a wide array of restaurants, from plate lunch houses to upscale Japanese bistros. It's on the table at every social gathering, from baby lūʻau to wedding receptions to memorial services. And like rubber slippers, "Eddie Would Go" bumper stickers and the ability to eat peas with chopsticks, it also serves as a subtle social marker, one more defining characteristic of who is and isn't "local." Got poke? You're headed in the right direction.

Virtually every supermarket now carries at least one version of the standard ʻahi-shoyu-onion variety, and several have entire refrigerator cases catering to a growing and diverse clientele. And poke is by no means limited to ʻahi. Depending on one's tastes, there's everything from the vegetarian tofu poke of Honolulu healthfood co-op Kokua Market to a goat poke that Tamura's Fine Wine and Liquors in Kaimukī has carried on at least one recent occasion. This, of course, is part of poke's allure: It's flexible.

Before we go any further, a note to the puzzled: It's not pronounced as the English-language "poke," like some sharp culinary jab in the belly. It's po-KAY, OK? And no, chef Sam Choy didn't invent the dish—but he certainly deserves a substantial portion of the credit for boosting its presence at the table, both in Hawaiʻi and far beyond. It's been on the menu in his restaurants since he opened his first place on the Big Island in 1981.

Ask Sam about the dish, and it's clear that this isn't just a simple pūpū plate he's talking about. According to Pukui and Elbert's *Hawaiian Dictionary*, "poke" itself merely means "to slice, [or] cut crosswise into pieces." But the modern version of poke; that is, a wide range of raw (usually) seafood (mostly), cut into cubes and dressed with a broad range of sauces and spices, draws on a recipe that is centuries-old.

"Poke is a true dish from Hawai'i, like our music and our dance and our culture," Sam asserts. "I put the food in the same category as all of those."

Indeed, most historians note that while early Hawaiians regularly ate raw seafood, they rarely if ever did so without some sort of seasoning—with, at the minimum, some amount of sea salt.

"Large fish eaten raw were prepared by mashing the flesh with the fingers, a process called lomi," writes Margaret Titcomb in her 1972 book *Native Use of Fish In Hawai'i*. "[T]he object being to soften and allow the salt or other flavor to penetrate. If the flesh [was] not soft enough for lomi ... it was cut into small slices or chunks, or left whole, and called i'a nahu pu (fish to bite into)." In the 1983 collection *'Olelo No'eau: Hawaiian Proverbs and Poetical Sayings*, linguist and historian Mary Kawena Pukui makes mention of a dish called i'a ho'omelu (literally "to allow to begin to spoil"), in which certain fish—most notably the small- to medium-sized, brightly colored reef fish known as hinalea—were allowed to decompose slightly and then seasoned with salt, 'inamona (a kukui nut relish) and chili pepper.

And then there is also William Ellis, Captain Cook's surgeon, who wrote that Hawaiians ate fish "raw, guts, scales and all; and use an immoderate quantity of salt with them." The scales may have been an exaggeration, but as Titcomb confirms, virtually every part of the fish was consumed—including, if one so desired, a certain amount of the fish's blood in the mix.

As for poke proper, Sam Choy has spent a great deal of time researching the method at its source(s)—an undertaking that has drawn him along on a wide arc through the Pacific.

"About five years ago, I took the tour: You gotta start off with South America because, basically, that's the first sign of raw fish out there—you know, they've got seviche," he says, pointing to the preparation in which seafood is soaked in lemon or lime juice until it is "cooked" firm by the juice's citric acid.

As I came around to Rapa Nui and even into Pitcairn, I found that there were traces of poke there, too. Rapa Nui was like the old Hawaiian poke, where they cut up the aku (skipjack) and then put the innards and the fish blood into it. And then, when you come around the horn and into the Tuamotus and Tahiti, you come across poisson cru, where the raw fish is also cooked with lime juice. Throughout Fiji—where a preparation similar to poisson cru is called kokoda—and other parts of the South Pacific, you find a little more Island-style poke, where they're using a lot of reef fish.

And then, of course, you come to Hawai'i, where traditional poke consisted mainly of reef fish, sea salt gathered off the shoreline, 'inamona for flavoring, all sorts of limu (seaweed)—manauea, līpe'epe'e, limu kohu—and the chili pepper to spice it up. And as the canoes began to run out to deeper water, they got to using aku and 'ahi—this was the basic poke.

As Sam goes on to explain, this basic preparation has metamorphosed over the years, the bare-bones, salt-kukui-seaweed mix expanding to include an ever-widening variety of ingredients. "It's really a no-brainer," he says. "It shifted with time: In terms of the American culture's contribution to Hawaiian cuisine, all they brought to the table was salt and pepper. Our backyard is Asia—if you look at the really 'ono pokes, they're basically like a teriyaki sauce, with the exception of sesame seed oil. Take a soy sauce base, add sesame seeds, put a little touch of sugar and then add green and white onions, hot peppers and mix it—that's pretty much the basis for the Asian influence over time."

Sam doesn't begrudge the influx of new ingredients and preparations. In fact, he embraces them: "You know, a lot of people have taken it beyond," he says, when asked how he feels about various liberties taken with the dish. "I've seen cubed mango poke; I've seen beef poke in Japan. We just want to make sure that poke gets a fair shot, you know what I'm saying? When you look at sushi and sashimi, they're pretty much household names in the world today. But when you talk about poke, it's still like a little whisper out there in the world."

The many and varied recipes included here come from the world's first poke cookbook, *Sam Choy's Poke*, which appeared in 1999. These favorite recipes— some developed by Sam, some gathered from Hawai'i poke aficionados—will give you a taste of the delicious ways that poke is prepared throughout the Islands. Enjoy!

—Stu Dawrs

TRADITIONAL
POKE

The original poke preparations have a flavor
that duplicates the ocean, with abundant
seaweeds and sea salt. The nuttiness of 'inamona
accentuates the natural sweetness
of the fish. This is poke in its purest and
most primal form.

Straight Hawaiian-Style 'Inamona Poke

Serves 6-1/2 cup servings

1 pound very fresh raw aku or 'ahi, cut in bite-size cubes
1 small ball *limu kohu*, about 1/2 cup
1 teaspoon *'inamona* or to taste
1 Hawaiian red chile pepper or bird pepper, minced
Salt to taste

Rinse and chop limu kohu. In a mixing bowl, combine all ingredients.

A Note on the Ingredients

Limu kohu is a species of edible red seaweed. 'Inamona is a condiment made of roasted, crushed and salted kukui nuts. Both limu kohu and 'inamona can be found in fish markets and Hawaiian delicatessens. (See Introduction for recommended seafood markets.) Other types of edible red seaweed may substitute for limu kohu – but seaweed of some kind must be used, as it has a distinctive iodine-accented flavor. If you can't find 'inamona, you can substitute 1-1/2 teaspoons cashew nuts, roasted, crushed and salted.

—Originally appeared in The Choy of Cooking

Helena Pali Opihi Limu Poke

Serves 36 (1 tablespoon servings)

This delicacy is served by the tablespoon at a lūʻau. ʻOpihi are limpets, which are also found in Oregon. The Oregon limpet has a hole inside. Theyʻre even tastier that Hawaiian ʻopihi.

2 cups shelled fresh ʻopihi (limpets)
Hawaiian salt for rinsing
1/2 cup rinsed and chopped limu huluhulu waena
    (dark red seaweed)
1/8 teaspoon Hawaiian salt

Shell ʻopihi by scooping the meat out of the shell with a spoon. Place shelled ʻopihi in a colander, sprinkle with Hawaiian salt and rinse under cold running water. Repeat this process two or three times until slime is removed.

Fold together raw cleaned ʻopihi and limu. Sprinkle with 1/8 teaspoon Hawaiian salt and fold again. Chill until served.

—*Originally appeared in* The Choy of Cooking

Old-Fashioned Hawaiian Poke

Makes 10 cups

3 pounds fresh 'ahi (yellowfin tuna)
1 cup limu lipoa (See note below)
1 tablespoon 'alaea salt (red Hawaiian salt)
3 tablespoons 'inamona (See note below)
4 Hawaiian red chili peppers, seeded and chopped

Cut 'ahi into thumb-size chunks and place in a bowl.

Rinse and chop limu and mix together with the 'alaea salt, 'inamona, and chili peppers. Add to the 'ahi and mix well. Cover until ready to serve.

The poke is very attractive in a koa or other wooden bowl lined with ti leaves.

About limu lipoa
Limu lipoa is found off the shore of Lahaina, Maui. Its flavor is the essence of the ocean. Hawaiian people enjoy the freshness of 'ahi and lipoa together.

About 'inamona
'Inamona is crushed and roasted kukui nut, usually with salt added; you can substitute 4-1/2 tablespoons crushed, roasted and salted cashew nuts for this poke.

—*Submitted by Julie Franco*

SHOYU (SOY SAUCE) POKE

Shoyu (Japanese Soy Sauce) is a favorite seasoning in Hawai'i. Here it has a starring role, adding a bright and zesty flavor to poke.

Poke in Flight

Makes about 8 cups

The addition of flying fish roe added at the very end is a Japanese touch. The crunchiness of the roe combined with the crispness of the seaweed makes for a real "taste treat".

4 tablespoons macadamia nut oil
3 large garlic cloves, peeled and sliced
6 tablespoons Aloha shoyu
2 pounds fresh sashimi-grade 'ahi (yellowfin tuna)
1/2 cup minced Maui onion
1/2 cup minced green onions
2 teaspoons Maggi seasoning
4 tablespoons minced cilantro
1 cup rinsed and chopped ogo seaweed
2/3 cup tobiko (flying fish roe)
Your favorite hot sauce

In a small pan, heat the macadamia nut oil until smoking. Add the garlic and stir-fry until garlic turns dark brown. (Be careful not to burn garlic, as it will turn bitter.) Remove and discard the garlic; retain oil. Immediately add soy sauce to the oil, being careful to avoid splattering. Loosely cover the pan and turn the heat off; allow the mixture to slowly cool on the burner to room temperature.

Cut 'ahi into 3/4 inch cubes and combine all the remaining ingredients, except the tobiko and hot sauce. Add cooled oil mixture and toss; add tobiko and toss lightly. Serve hot sauce separately.

—*Submitted by Karl M. Tsukazaki*

Seared 'Ahi and Macadamia Poke

Makes 5 cups

1 pound block 'ahi
Vegetable oil for searing
1/2 cup chopped unsalted macadamia nuts
2 tablespoons chili pepper oil
5 tablespoons Aloha shoyu
1/4 cup chopped green onions
1/4 cup chopped onion
1 tomato, diced
1 cup rinsed and chopped ogo seaweed

Slice 'ahi into 3/4 inch strips. Add a light coat of oil to bottom of a skillet. Heat skillet to high and sear 'ahi lightly in hot frying pan- so center of 'ahi pieces are still raw to rare. Let 'ahi cool and cut into 3/4 inch cubes.

In a large bowl, combine 'ahi with 1/3 cup of the macadamia nuts, chili, pepper, oil, soy sauce, onion, tomato and ogo seaweed. Mix well and chill. Serve topped with remaining macadamia nuts for a garnish.

—Submitted by Roy T. Kaneko

Aku Poke with Shoyu

Makes about 7 cups

2 pounds fresh aku (skipjack tuna)
1 tablespoon Hawaiian salt
1/2 teaspoon 'inamona (See note)
1-1/2 tablespoons sesame oil
2 tablespoons oyster sauce
4 to 5 tablespoon Aloha shoyu
2 Hawaiian chili peppers, chopped
1/4 cup chopped green onions
1/4 cup chopped Maui onion
1-1/2 cups ogo seaweed (optional)

Cut the aku into 3/4-inch cubes; mix with Hawaiian salt and allow it to sit for 5 minutes. Add the remaining ingredients and mix thoroughly. Serve chilled.

Note:
'Inamona is crushed and roasted kukui nut, usually with salt added; you can substitute 3/4 teaspoons crushed cashew nuts for a similar taste.

—*Submitted by Tina Fujiwara*

Japanese-Style Poke

Makes about 4 cups

This poke is garnished with nasturtium flowers, which besides being tasty add a natural spiciness to the dish.

1 pound 'ahi (yellowfin tuna) filet
1 medium-size daikon (white icicle radish)
1 package (1/3 ounce) ajitsuke nori (hot)
4 tablespoons finely cut onion chives
3 Hawaiian chili peppers, or to taste
3/4 cup light Aloha shoyu
Nasturtium flowers for garnish

Cut 'ahi into 1/2 inch cubes. Place in medium-size bowl. Grate the daikon, as fine as can be done, and squeeze out all the excess water. Add to 'ahi and toss. Break up the nori into 1/2 to 1 inch pieces and sprinkle over 'ahi-daikon mixture.

Combine soy sauce, onion chives, and chili pepper and toss with 'ahi-daikon mixture. Cover and chill.

To serve, garnish with edible nasturtium flowers.

—*Submitted by Dean J. Okimoto*

Can't Get Enough Otaru Poke

Makes about 12 cups

"Otaru" is the Japanese word for a large aku, a member of the tuna family, also known as bonito. If you can't get otaru, a small aku, or some 'ahi with do just as well.

2 pounds otaru (large aku or skipjack tuna) or raw
    fish of your taste
2 tomatoes, chopped
2 cups rinsed and chopped limu seaweed of your choice
1 cup chopped onion
4 tablespoons Aloha shoyu
2 teaspoons sesame oil
1 Hawaiian chili pepper, minced, or 1 teaspoon red chili
    pepper flakes

Cut fish into 3/8 to 1/2 inch cubes and place in a large bowl. Add remaining ingredients and mix well. Chill until ice-cold and serve.

—*Originally appeared in* With Sam Choy

SPICY
POKE

Lovers of the chili pepper will enjoy
these wicked recipes.

Spicy Poke

Makes 6 cups

1 pound fresh 'ahi, in 1/2 inch pieces
1 medium tomato, in 1/4 inch dice
1 cup limu (red edible seaweed), chopped
1/2 cup onion, chopped
1 cup cucumber, in 1/4 inch dice
1/2 cup green onion, in 1/4 inch pieces
1-1/2 to 2 tablespoons Aloha shoyu
1 teaspoon sesame oil
1/2 teaspoon Hawaiian or bird chili pepper, seeded and minced
1 teaspoon *Kim Chee base**
Salt and pepper to taste

In a mixing bowl, combine all of the ingredients except the salt and pepper. Toss gently. Taste for seasoning, and adjust with salt and pepper if necessary. Be sure to keep the fish very cold.

*Kim Chee base, a red chili and garlic pickling brine for vegetables, may be found in Korean or Japanese markets. You may also substitute 1 teaspoon of Asian chili sauce and a dash of vinegar for the Kim Chee base.

—*Originally appeared in* The Choy of Seafood

Kim Chee Poke

Makes 4 cups

Kim Chee Marinade (See recipe opposite)
1/2 head won bok (Chinese cabbage or napa cabbage),
    cut in squares
1 Japanese cucumber, seeded and cut into cubes
Pinch Hawaiian salt
4 ounces Shutome (swordfish)
4 ounces 'ahi (yellowfin tuna)
12 ounces mung bean sprouts (about 3 cups)
White and black sesame seeds, for garnish

Massage Hawaiian salt into the cabbage and cucumber in separate containers. Allow to stand overnight covered at room temperature. Rinse and drain the next day.

Marinate vegetables for 2 hours in Kim Chee Marinade. Meanwhile cut the swordfish into 1/2 inch cubes and the 'ahi into 3/4 inch cubes.

Drain the cabbage and cucumber mixture and add the cubed fish and mix together. Serve poke over the bean sprouts. Garnish with white and black sesame seeds.

Kim Chee Marinade

1/2 package (about 1/2 ounce) Noh brand kim chee mix
1/4 cup water
1/4 teaspoon garlic, crushed into a puree
1/4 teaspoon ginger, crushed into a puree
1/4 teaspoon paprika
1/4 teaspoon cayenne pepper
1/4 teaspoon chili flakes

Mix ingredients together and let stand for 1 hour.

—*Submitted by Mark Mattos*

Red Hot and Blackened Poke

Makes about 3 cups

This California recipe coats the fish in peppers and sears it in a hot pan for a few seconds. The spiciness of the fish becomes spicier with the addition of the slaw and sambal marinade. Be sure the pan is so hot some smoke appears in order to effectively sear the fish with the spices.

10 ounces Sambal Marinade (See recipe on next page)
1 pound Chili Pepper Slaw (See recipe on next page)
1 pound swordfish filets
2 teaspoons salt
2 teaspoons cayenne pepper
2 tablespoons ground thyme leaves
2 tablespoons file powder

Clean swordfish by removing all blood line (the dark red meat near the bone), skin and sinew. Slice filets 1 inch thick. In a bowl, mix together salt, cayenne pepper, thyme leaves and file powder.

Heat a cast iron skillet over a high heat until very hot. Dredge the swordfish filets in the spice mixture and place them into the cast iron pan. Sear for 45 to 60 seconds on each side. Remove from heat and cool to room temperature. Cut into 1 inch diamonds. Marinate the finished swordfish in a few ounces of the Sambal Marinade for 2 to 4 hours.

Combine the Sambal Marinade with the slaw and allow to marinate for 15 minutes. Combine the marinated blackened swordfish with the slaw. Serve immediately.

continued on next page

Sambal Marinade

2 tablespoons brown sugar
2 tablespoons Aloha shoyu
4 tablespoons lemon juice
1/3 cup skinned and julienned red onion
1/4 cup vegetable oil

Combine all marinade ingredients and mix until sugar is completely dissolved.

Chili Pepper Slaw

1/4 cup shredded carrot
2 (1-1/2 ounces) Anaheim peppers, seeded and slivered
4 tablespoons sambal (Asian chili paste)
2 cups shredded green cabbage
1 red bell pepper, seeded and slivered
1 cup coarsely chopped macadamia nuts

Combine all the vegetables gently in a bowl.

—*Submitted by Philip L. Costner*

SHELLFISH AND OCTOPUS POKE

Poke works with all sorts of seafood, from sweet prawns to delicate oysters. Be sure to use the freshest available.

"Ogo," You Go, I Go Oysters

24 oysters on the half shells

24 live oysters
1 cup granulated sugar
1 cup Aloha shoyu
1 Hawaiian chili pepper, minced
1 tablespoon peeled and minced fresh ginger
3/4 cup rice vinegar
1/2 Maui (sweet) onion, very thinly sliced
2 tablespoons minced green onions
2 tablespoons sesame seeds
1 pound rinsed and chopped ogo seaweed

To prepare oysters, scrub all the dirt from the oyster shells with a brush under cold running water. With a towel, hold an oyster with one hand while inserting the point of a blunt knife into the hinge of the shell. Twist the knife until the shell pops open. Repeat for remaining oysters. Use the knife to loosen oyster flesh from the shell. Rinse oysters under cold running water, drain, and serve, on the half shell, on a platter.

In a large mixing bowl, combine sugar, soy sauce, chili peppers, ginger and rice vinegar; mix well until sugar is dissolved. Add onions, sesame seeds and ogo.

Scoop small amounts of ogo mix onto the oysters.

—*Originally appeared in* The Choy of Seafood

Poke Crab Medley

Serves 4

This recipe was the Grand Prize Winner in the First Annual Sam Choy Festival. A very simple and easy-to-prepare recipe, the combination of 'alaea salt, chili pepper flakes and 'inamona brings out a delicious flavor to this whole crab poke.

Red and green ogo seaweed (as desired)
1 Kona crab
2 white crabs
2 'a'ama crabs (black rock crabs)
2 tablespoons 'inamona (see note)
1 teaspoon red chili pepper flakes
1 tablespoon 'alaea salt (red Hawaiian salt)

Rinse and chop ogo seaweed and chill for later use. Remove the back shell and gills from all of the crabs. Do not remove the claws or legs. Wash and drain the crabs. Chop the shoulder of the Kona crab into 8 pieces; white crabs into 4 pieces each; 'a'ama crabs into 2 pieces each.

Combine the 'inamona, 'alaea salt, and chili pepper flakes and sprinkle on the crabs. Serve crabs over chilled green ogo seaweed and garnish with sprigs of red ogo.

Note:
'Inamona is crushed and roasted kukui nut, usually with salt added; substitute 3 tablespoons crushed, roasted and salted cashew nuts for a similar taste. —Submitted by Karen L.U.

Da Kine Poke Supreme

Serves 24

2 cups raw 'ahi, cubed
1 cup opihi, or poached scallops, or cooked mussels
6 whole crabs, cleaned and lighted salted, quartered
2 lbs cooked octopus, thinly sliced
1/2 cup ogo, chopped
1 cup limu wawae'iole (rat's feet seaweed or miru),
     coarsely chopped
2 tomatoes, chopped
2 cups cucumbers, chopped
1 cup onion, chopped
6 Tbsp. Aloha Shoyu
2 tsp. sesame oil
1 tsp. red pepper flakes, or 1 Hawaiian chili pepper

Mix ingredients well and chill until ice-cold.

—*Originally appeared in* With Sam Choy

Korean-Style Tako Poke

Makes 13 cups

2 pounds ogo seaweed
1 pound octopus (tako)
1 Maui (or other sweet) onions
1/2 cup chopped green onions
1 cup rice vinegar
1/2 cup Aloha shoyu
1/2 cup granulated sugar
3 tablespoons roasted sesame seeds
2 tablespoons kochu jang (Korean chili paste)
1 teaspoon peeled and minced fresh ginger
2 teaspoons minced fresh garlic

Rinse ogo and cut in 2 inch lengths. Refrigerate.

To cook already cleaned octopus (*see note*), bring enough water to cover octopus to a boil. Place octopus into boiling water and return the water to a rolling boil. Cook for 2 to 3 minutes. Drain and then plunge octopus into cold water to prevent over-cooking. Slice into thin slices.

In a mixing bowl, combine remaining ingredients and mix thoroughly. Add in chilled ogo and cooked octopus and toss. This poke is ready to serve or refrigerate for later use at tailgate parties or backyard barbecues.

To Clean a Fresh Octopus:
Turn the head inside out, and remove the ink sac and internal organs and rinse thoroughly. To tenderize the octopus, you can freeze it overnight or pound or massage it until tender.

—*Originally appeared in* The Choy of Cooking

Hana Hou Poke

Makes about 8 cups

2 pounds fresh aku (skipjack tuna)
1-1/2 tablespoons Hawaiian salt with 'inamona (see note)
1 cup rinsed and chopped limu kohu (red seaweed)
3 hawaiian chili peppers, minced
2 tablespoons light Aloha shoyu
2 cups 'opihi (limpets), 25 cent piece size
1 cup chopped green onions
10 cherry tomatoes, sliced in half

Cut aku into 3/4 inch cubes and combine with Hawaiian salt, 'inamona, limu kohu, Hawaiian chili peppers and soy sauce; cover and marinate in the refrigerator.

Remove the 'opihi from the shell. Using a colander, massage the 'opihi with Hawaiian salt and rinse with cold running water and repeat two more times until slime is removed. Add a small handful of Hawaiian salt to the colander, mix it into the 'opihi, and place a bowl under the colander and marinate 'opihi 1 hour in the refrigerator.

After a couple of hours, combine the aku poke and 'opihi together in a large bowl. Add the green onions and cherry tomatoes.

Note:
If 'inamona is not available; use crushed, roasted and slated cashew nuts instead for a similar taste. —*Submitted by Trini Catillo*

TOFU
AND
VEGETABLE
POKE

Tofu is also delicious when paired with
poke seasons and vegetarians and non-vegetarians
alike will be delighted with the sweet potato
poke, too. Also included is a recipe that combines
the charms of both 'ahi and tofu.

Mauka Poke

Makes about 6 cups

This vegetarian poke features potato in a coconut, soy and 'inamona sauce. Very unique.

1 Okinawan purple sweet potato (about 2 cups cubed)
1 orange yam (about 2 cups cubed)
1 yellow sweet potato (about 2 cups cubed)
1/2 teaspoon peeled and grated fresh ginger
1/2 teaspoon chopped garlic
1/2 teaspoon 'inamona (see note)
1 teaspoon crushed red pepper
2 tablespoons shredded coconut
2 tablespoons Aloha shoyu
1/4 cup thinly julienned pepeiao akua (tree fungus)
1/4 cup coconut milk
Chopped green onions, for garnish

Peel and cube the Okinawan sweet potato, orange yam and yellow sweet potato and steam them until al dente. Place potatoes and yam in a large bowl and add remaining ingredients. Mix thoroughly to coat potatoes well. Garnish poke with chopped green onions.

Note:
'Inamona is crushed and roasted kukui nut, usually with salt added. For a similar taste, use 1-1/2 teaspoons chopped roasted and salted cashew nuts. —*Submitted by Peter Lloyd Pao*

'Ahi Poke Furikake

Makes about 5 cups

1 pound very fresh 'ahi (yellowfin tuna)
1 pound firm tofu, drained
1 tablespoon peeled and grated fresh ginger
5 tablespoons furikake (dried seaweed flakes blended with seasoned sesame seeds)
1/4 cup macadamia nuts, roasted and mashed with 'alaea salt (to taste)
1 cup rinsed and chopped ogo seaweed
1 Hawaiian chili pepper, minced
3 tablespoons Aloha shoyu
1/2 cup chopped fresh chives

Cut 'ahi and tofu into bite-size pieces. Add grated ginger, furikake, macadamia nuts and ogo. Mix chili pepper with soy sauce and add to the fish mixture. Mix well.

Garnish with chives and chill for 20 minutes before eating.

—*Submitted by Kimberlee Tong*

Volcano Tofu Poke

Makes 2 cups

1 block (20 ounces) firm tofu, drained
1/2 teaspoon brown sugar
1/2 teaspoon red chili pepper flakes or minced Hawaiian
    chili pepper
1 teaspoon sesame oil
1/2 inch piece ginger, roasted and finely chopped
5 garlic cloves, thinly sliced and fried until brown
1/2 cup Aloha shoyu
1 tablespoon rinsed and chopped ogo seaweed
2 sprigs chopped fresh cilantro
2 stalks green onions or scallions

Cut tofu into 3/4 inch cubes and place into a bowl. In a separate bowl, combine the brown sugar, chili pepper flakes, sesame oil, ginger, garlic and soy sauce; mix together. Toss in the tofu and ogo.

Place poke on a plate and garnish with cilantro, green onions or scallions.

—Submitted by Surt Thammountha

Elegant Tofu Poke

Makes 4 to 5 cups

This dish uses the classical Chinese method of serving steamed or poached fish with a heated oil and soy sauce combination poured over the fish prior to serving.

1 block (20 ounces) firm tofu
4 tablespoons macadamia nut oil
3 large garlic cloves, sliced
6 tablespoons Aloha shoyu
1 tablespoon peeled and finely minced fresh ginger
2 tablespoons minced fresh cilantro
3/4 cup minced Maui (or other sweet) onion
3/4 cup minced green onions
1 cup rinsed and chopped ogo seaweed

Sliced tofu crosswise into 4 pieces and place flat on doubled sheets of paper towels to absorb the water. Place in the refrigerator. Allow at least 2 hours prior to poke preparation for tofu to drain adequately.

In a deep skillet or wok, heat the macadamia nut oil until smoking. Add the garlic and stir-fry until garlic turns dark brown. Discard garlic (used only to flavor the oil) and

continued on next page

immediately add soy sauce to the oil (use extreme caution because the soy-oil mixture will splatter). Loosely cover the pot, turn off the heat, and let mixture slowly cool on burner to room temperature.

Place all the remaining ingredients, except tofu, in a large mixing bowl. Pour the cooled oil mixture over and toss lightly to combine well. Set aside.

Slice the tofu pieces to 3/4 inch cubes. Arrange in a single layer in a shallow serving dish. Spread the onion-soy sauce oil mixture evenly over the tofu. Serve immediately.

—*Submitted by Karl M. Tsukazaki*

SEVICHE
STYLE

Seviche is an unusual preparation that "cooks" fish and seafood with an acid solution, usually lime or lemon juice. This type of dish comes from Latin American countries as well as Tahiti, where it is called "poisson cru."

Hawaiian Ota

Makes about 6 cups

1-1/2 cups fresh raw pale-fleshed fish (such as grouper or
    sea bass)
Juice of 6 limes (about 1/3 cup)
1 teaspoon Hawaiian salt
1 cup finely chopped onion
1 cup seeded and finely chopped cucumber
1 cup seeded and finely chopped firm ripe tomato
1/2 cup fresh green chili, seeded, pulp removed and
    minced to 1/8 inch
1-1/2 cups pure undiluted coconut cream (preferably
    Mendonca brand frozen coconut cream)

Cut fish into 1/2 inch cubes and combine with lime juice (do
not use lemon juice). Stir lightly and until all the fish cubes
are well coated with lime juice. Refrigerate in a covered bowl
for at least 2 hours or overnight.

Add salt to the marinated fish and stir until the salt is
dissolved. More of less salt may be used according to taste.
Add the chopped vegetables. Other finely chopped fresh
vegetables; raw or blanched (for example, carrots or peas)
also may be used, either in combination with the above
vegetables or as substitutes.

Add the coconut cream and blend all the ingredients and chill.
Serve cold.

—*Submitted by Nahekeaopono Ka'iuwailani*

Hawaiian-Style Crawfish Seviche Poke

Makes about 5 cups

4 pounds live crawfish
1 sprig fresh cilantro, chopped
1 teaspoon chili oil
4 to 6 Hawaiian chili peppers, chopped
Juice of 2 limes (about 2 tablespoons)
1 Maui (or other sweet) onions, chopped
1 to 2 tomatoes, chopped

Fill a large pot two-thirds full of water and bring to a boil. Submerge live crawfish and boil for 3 to 5 minutes. Remove from water and plunge immediately into ice water to stop the cooking process. Shell when cool.

In a bowl, combine crawfish meat and remaining ingredients and mix. Cover and refrigerate overnight.

—*Submitted by Lance Caspary*

Fiesta Poke

Makes 8 to 10 cups

1 pound fresh snapper
Juice of 2 limes (about 2 tablespoons)
1/4 pound octopus
1/4 pound scallops (30 to 40 per pound)
5 firm tomatoes, seeded and diced
1 medium Maui (or other sweet) chopped
1/3 cup fresh cilantro, finely chopped (use only the leaves)
1/3 cup finely chopped green onions
1 fresh chili pepper, seeded and finely chopped (optional)
1/2 teaspoon salt or to taste
Sliced avocadoes

Cut the snapper into bite-size cubes and place in a bowl. Use just enough lime juice to cover the snapper and "cook" the fish by marinating it overnight.

Cut octopus and scallops into bite-size cubes and mix with tomatoes, onion, cilantro, green onions and remaining lime juice. Add chili peppers if desired. Toss well. Add salt. Refrigerate for at least 3 hours. Serve cold with avocado slices.

—Submitted by Liza Jang-Che

POKE
WITH A
TWIST

Many variations of poke are possible. The recipes in this section explore exciting possibilities—there is even a recipe here for poke made with beef!

Tropical Island Poke

Serves 4-6

An 'ahi's size makes a big difference in the quality and texture of the meat. Small 'ahi have pinkish meat, while larger 'ahi have a deeper red color. The larger the fish, the higher the fat content, a desirable attribute for raw fish and broiling recipes.

I like coming up with interesting flavor combinations that REALLY work. The coconut milk and mango dramatically put the "tropical" in this Island poke. It's an interesting combination of textures —'ahi, mango cubes—soaked in shoyu, sesame oil, and coconut milk. It's a real blend of the South Pacific, Eastern Pacific, and, of course, Hawai'i.

1 pound fresh 'ahi fillet, cut into 1/2-inch cubes
2 teaspoons sesame oil
3 tablespoons Aloha shoyu
1 teaspoon fresh garlic, finely chopped
2 fresh Hawaiian chili peppers, finely chopped
1/2 cup coconut milk
1 cup mango, 1/2-inch cubes
1/2 cup red bell pepper, 1/2-inch cubes
1/4 cup cilantro, chopped
2 tablespoons lemon juice
salt to taste
Cilantro, chopped, for garnish

Combine all ingredients in a bowl, except 'ahi. Mix well. Add 'ahi to mixture, and marinate at least 1 hour before serving. Garnish with chopped cilantro.

—*Originally appeared in* The Choy of Seafood

Kelly's Special

Makes 8 to 10 cups

During the late 60's and early 70's we regularly ate at Mama Loki's Hawaiian Restaurant on Kekauliki Street. Lomi aku and lomi salmon were standard fare on the menu. One of the regulars, a diver named Kelly Ahuna, used to order a dish of each and combine the two at his table. Naturally, we were curious and asked to taste the concoction. The combination became so popular that Mama Loki named it after Kelly.

1 pound aku (skipjack tuna)
1/2 pound salted salmon
2 pounds tomatoes (cherry or plum)
1/2 cup green onions
Sea salt, chili peppers and 'inamona (see note) to taste
1 medium Maui (or other sweet) onion
Limu (seaweed) of your choice as garnish

Cut aku into 3/4 inch cubes and massage (lomi) them by hand. Set aside. Rinse the salmon and massage it by hand. Do not remove the skins from the cherry or plum tomatoes. Break the tomatoes into small pieces and crush by hand. Cut the green onions into 1 inch lengths and crush using a mortar and pestle.

Combine all the ingredients except the seaweed and chill before serving. If you can't wait, add ice cubes. For a juicier poke, add 3/4 cup water. To serve, garnish with seaweed.

—*Submitted by Ted Farm*

'Ahi Poke with Lemon Grass

Makes about 3 cups

1 pound fresh raw 'ahi (yellowfin tuna)
White pepper to taste
Pinch of crushed chili pepper
1/2 stalk lemon grass, finely minced
1 teaspoon Asian chili paste
1/4 red onion, sliced thin
1/4 cup chopped green onions
5 to 6 slivered fresh mint leaves
Juice of 1/2 lime (about 1-1/2 teaspoons)
Salt to taste
1/4 cup chopped fresh cilantro

Cut 'ahi into 3/4 inch cubes and place in a bowl. Add white pepper, crushed chili, minced lemon grass, chili paste, red and green onions, mint leaves and lime juice and add to fish. Toss together lightly and add salt if desired.

Chill for 1 hour and place on a serving dish. Serve this poke chilled and garnish with cilantro.

—Submitted by Charlie Chintam

Wok-Seared Kajiki Poke with Grilled Pineapple Salsa

Makes 7 cups

Grilled Pineapple Salsa (see recipe below)
2 pounds kajiki (marlin)
2 tablespoons Cajun spice
1/4 cup salad oil
1/4 cup chili oil
Salt and pepper to taste
5 sprigs cilantro
Taro chips (optional)

Cut Kajiki into 3/4 inch cubes and mix together with Cajun spice, salad oil, chili oil, salt and pepper. Allow to sit at room temperature for 30 minutes. Heat wok, add poke ingredients, and sear until done medium rare. Drain excess oil.

Toss with Grilled Pineapple Salsa. Garnish with cilantro sprigs and serve with taro chips if desired.

Grilled Pineapple Salsa
3 tablespoons sliced olives
2 tablespoons liliko'i (passion fruit) juice concentrate
1/4 cup cooked black beans
2 jalapeno peppers, sliced
2 thin slices pineapple, grilled and diced
3/4 cup diced avocado
Juice and zest of 1 lime
1 cup homemade or prepared tomato salsa

Mix all the ingredients. Refrigerate for 6 hours.

—Submitted by Patrick Uchima

Green Onion and Cilantro Pesto Poke

Makes 16 cups

This version of pesto uses cilantro and macadamia nuts to create a delicious and unusual seasoning for the poke.

Cilantro Pesto (see recipe below)
2-1/2 pounds very fresh 'ahi (yellowfin tuna)
1/4 cup coarse salt

Cut 'ahi into 3/8 to 1/2 inch cubes. Add salt and blend well by hand. After the salt has dissolved into the 'ahi, add the Cilantro Pesto and mix thoroughly. Chill for 1 to 2 hours and serve.

Cilantro Pesto
1/2 pound diced green onions (about 2 cups)
1/2 pound diced fresh cilantro (about 10 cups loosely packed)
1/2 cup chopped macadamia nuts
3/4 cup salad oil

In a food processor, combine the green onions, cilantro, macadamia nuts and salad oil. Process until pureed and well combined.

—*Submitted by W. Bones Yuen*

Dad's Ho Mei Poke

Makes 4 cups

This traditional Chinese preparation of fish is accentuated by dry mustard, a splash of vodka and sesame and peanut oil.

Dipping Sauce (see recipe on next page)
1 teaspoon peanut oil
1 pound fresh snapper, thinly sliced and refrigerated
1-1/2 inch peeled and finely slivered fresh ginger
1/2 cup finely slivered green onions
1/2 cup finely slivered Maui (or other sweet) onion
1/4 cup finely slivered lemon zest
1/4 teaspoon ground white pepper
1/2 teaspoon salt
1 tablespoon sesame oil
2 tablespoons Aloha shoyu
Splash of vodka
1/4 cup fresh cilantro leaves
1 tablespoon toasted black sesame seeds

Heat the peanut oil, but do not let it smoke. Cook to room temperature. (This procedure intensifies the flavor of the peanut oil.)

continued on next page

In a large bowl, place the snapper and half of the ginger, green onions, onion and lemon rind. Add salt, sesame oil, soy sauce and vodka into the same bowl. Toss together well. Refrigerate for 1 hour.

Serve the poke sprinkled with the cilantro and toasted sesame seeds. The remaining ginger root, green onions, onion and lemon rind may be served as condiments for the poke along with the dipping sauce.

Dipping Sauce
1 tablespoon dry mustard (such as Colman's)
3 tablespoons water
1/4 teaspoon peanut oil
1 teaspoon Aloha shoyu
2 teaspoons lemon juice
Dash of sesame oil

Mix the dry mustard with water. Stir in the soy sauce, peanut oil, lemon juice and sesame oil.

—Submitted by Liza Jang-Che

Marinated Steak Poke

Makes about 7 cups

Poke using flank steak as the main ingredient instead of seafood presents a unique example of how the poke concept can be expanded.

Sam's Teriyaki Marinade (see recipe on next page)
1-1/2 pounds flank steak
1/2 teaspoon red pepper flakes
1 tablespoon sesame seeds, roasted
1 tablespoon sesame oil
2-1/2 teaspoons chili oil
1 garlic clove, peeled and minced
1 green onion top, sliced
1 small Maui (or other sweet) onion, thinly sliced
1 cup chopped Japanese cucumber

Marinate the steak for 6 hours in Sam's Teriyaki Marinade. Grill the steak slowly until rare to medium rare, being careful not to get it too brown. Cool and refrigerate until cold.

Cut the steak into 1/2 inch cubes and add the remaining ingredients. Mix well. Return to the refrigerator for 1 hour before serving.

continued on next page

Sam's Teriyaki Marinade

1/8 teaspoon white pepper
1 cup granulated sugar
2 tablespoons thinly sliced green onions
1/4 cup minced ginger
1-1/2 cups Aloha shoyu

Combine all the marinade ingredients and blend well.

—*Submitted by Julia Paquin*

COOKED
POKE

Though poke is traditionally a raw seafood
dish—the flavors lend themselves
well to cooked preparations, as the following
imaginative dishes prove.

Poke My Way

Makes 1-1/2 cups poke filling

This recipe hails from the island of Kaua'i. It incorporates rice vinegar, Thai sweet chili sauce, coconut milk and taro leaves rolled in a spring roll wrapper and deep fried.

2 tablespoons chopped blanched lū'au leaf (young taro leaf)
    or spinach leaves
6 tablespoons sweet chili sauce
4 tablespoons rice vinegar
Salad oil as desired
1 teaspoon sesame oil
4 tablespoons coconut milk
2 tablespoons ginger, finely minced
2 tablespoons minced onion
2 tablespoons chopped green onions
Hawaiian salt to taste
4 ounces 'ahi (yellowfin tuna)
Spring roll wrappers
2 eggs, beaten

To blanch lū'au leaf, remove stem from lū'au leaf and blanch in boiling water for 3 minutes. Strain in colander. Set aside.

Mix the sweet chili and rice wine vinegar. Set aside for dipping sauce.

In a saucepan, heat the salad oil and sesame oil together. Add the cooked lū'au leaf, coconut milk, ginger, onions and Hawaiian salt. Cook until all the ingredients are mixed well and tender. Set aside and cool.

Dice the 'ahi and mix with coconut-onion mixture. Place mixture in the spring roll wrappers and roll; brush egg wash along seams to close.

In a deep heavy skillet or wok, heat sesame-salad oil to high. Fry spring rolls a few at a time until golden brown. Drain briefly on paper towels. Allow oil to return to sizzling temperature before adding a new batch of spring rolls to prevent from overcooking the 'ahi.

When all spring rolls are fried, serve with sweet chili-vinegar dipping sauce.

—*Submitted by Rafael Camarillo*

Cold-Smoked Cured Albacore Poke

Makes 4 to 6 cups

Smoking the fish over mesquite wood (kiawe), guava or other hardwood adds dimension to the poke.

1 pound albacore (tombo 'ahi)
Curing Salt (see recipe on opposite page)
1/8 teaspoon pepper
1 teaspoon toasted sesame seeds
1 teaspoon minced lemon grass
1/2 teaspoon fish sauce
1 tablespoon oyster sauce
1 tablespoon kim chee base
1 tablespoon olive oil
1 tablespoon sesame oil
1 teaspoon Aloha shoyu
1 tablespoon chopped Maui (or other sweet) onion
1 stalk chopped green onions
1 cucumber, diced
1 ripe tomato, diced
1 green tomato, diced
1/2 cup rinsed and chopped ogo seaweed
1 Hawaiian chili pepper, chopped

Slice albacore into 3/4-inch filets. Heavily coat the filets with the Curing Salt and place them in a zip-lock bag. Cure in the refrigerator for at least 3 days under a weight.

Cold smoke the filets over Kiawe, guava, or any wet hardwood shavings for 3 to 4 hours.

Cut the fish in to bite-size pieced and mix well with the other ingredients and refrigerate for at least 2 hours before serving.

Curing Salt
1/2 cup kosher salt
1 tablespoon brown sugar
1/8 teaspoon white pepper

Combine well.

—Submitted by Glen K. Lee

Sam Choy's World Famous Fried Marlin Poke

Serves 4

When I cook fish, I do it Chinese-style, by quickly searing it on high heat to seal in flavor and moisture; it's one of the secrets that makes the fish I serve at my restaurants taste so good.

20 ounces fresh raw marlin (see note)
4 teaspoons Aloha shoyu
1 cup chopped onion
4 teaspoons chopped green onions
1 cup rinsed and chopped ogo seaweed
4 teaspoons sesame oil
1 tablespoon vegetable oil
4 cups bean sprouts, chopped cabbage, or assorted
    fresh greens

Cut marlin into bite-size cubes about 3/4 inch in size. Place cubes in a mixing bowl with soy sauce, onions, ogo and sesame oil. Mix well.

In a hot wok, add oil and quickly sear the fish. Cook only for about a minute, keeping the centers of the marlin cubes raw. To serve, divide bean sprouts, chopped cabbage or greens into individual plates and top with fried marlin poke.

Note:
For this recipe, no other fish works as well as marlin.

—*Originally appeared in* With Sam Choy

Poke Sausage

Makes about 5 cups poke sausage mix.

This poke sausage retains its shape because it is steamed. Allow adequate time for the mixture to season prior to steaming, as it adds to the taste of the sausage. The use of shichimi togarashi and cilantro provide a hint of Asian influence in this poke created by a Japanese chef.

1 pound fresh 'ahi (yellowfin tuna), finely ground in a
    food processor
12 hokkigai (surf clams)
1/4 cup coarsely chopped macadamia nuts
2 tablespoons finely chopped fresh cilantro
2 tablespoons peeled and finely chopped fresh ginger
2 cloves garlic, finely chopped
1 tablespoon shichimi togarashi (seven spice seasoning)
Black pepper to taste
1 cup mayonnaise
Sea salt to taste
Aloha shoyu to taste
Sesame oil for frying
1 lemon, cut into wedges

Clean and thinly slice hokkigai and combine with 'ahi; mix. To the bowl, add macadamia nuts, cilantro, ginger, garlic, shichimi, black pepper and mayonnaise and mix thoroughly. Add the sea salt and soy sauce to taste. Using plastic wrap, form the 'ahi mixture into a sausage shape and steam the sausage for 10 minutes on plastic wrap, or until firm. Let it cool in the refrigerator.

In a large pan, heat the sesame oil. Slice the sausage diagonally in 1/6 inch pieces. Fry both sides until crispy. Drain on paper towels.

To serve, place the poke sausage on a large plate and add the lemon wedges on the side. Serve immediately.

—*Submitted by Karl M. Tsukazaki*

Macadamia Nut Encrusted 'Ahi Poke

Makes 8 cups

Macadamia nuts, an Island favorite, are used to coat the fish that is seared in a pan for a few seconds. After the fish is quickly seared, it is refrigerated to cool it down, and stop the cooking process. Besides the macadamia nuts and oil used for cooking the fish, the only other seasonings are the onion, seaweed and salt which makes this recipe very easy to prepare and one which macadamia nut lovers will thoroughly enjoy.

9 ounces unsalted macadamia nuts, finely chopped
2 pounds fresh 'ahi (yellowfin tuna)
3 tablespoons macadamia nut oil
6 paper towels soaked in ice water and squeezed
2 cups rinsed ogo seaweed, cut into 1/4 inch lengths
1 cup finely chopped Maui (or other sweet) onions
Hawaiian salt to taste

Cut 'ahi into 1/2 inch thick slices. Coat both sides of the 'ahi with crushed nuts, lightly pressing the nuts to adhere them to the filets.

Heat the macadamia nut oil to medium high heat in a non-stick pan. Carefully fry the coated filets for 15 to 30 seconds on each side. The macadamia nuts should be golden brown with only about 1/16 inch of the filet cooked on each side. Chill quickly by placing the cooked filets on the chilled paper towels. Place more chilled towels on top of the filets. Place the 'ahi and the paper towels in the freezer to further chill for about 30 minutes.

In a mixing bowl, add the ogo and onions and toss well. Slice the 'ahi filets into 1/2 inch cubes. Add to the ogo-onion mixture and salt to taste.

—Submitted by Hideaki "Santa" Miyoshi

POKE GLOSSARY

A

'A'ama Crab:
Hawaiian name for an edible black rock crab. This crab has small pinchers, a carapace about 3 inches wide, and is often eaten raw.

'Ahi:
Hawaiian name for yellowfin of bigeye tuna. Also called shibi in Japanese. When the term 'ahi is used, it is assumed that fresh tuna, rather than canned, is meant.

Ajitsuke Nori:
Nori sheets that are seasoned with soy sauce and sugar. Some are further seasoned with chilies—these are labeled as "hot" ajitsuke nori. See NORI.

'Alaea Salt:
A coarse sea salt that is colored with an orange-red natural clay.

Al Dente:
Italian phrase meaning cooked until just tender – still offering slight resistance to the bite.

Aku:
The Hawaiian word for skipjack or bonito tuna. This fish is often eaten raw as an appetizer.

C

Chili Oil:
sesame oil flavored with hot chili peppers. This can be purchased in Asian markets and should be kept refrigerated once opened.

Chili Paste:
a condiment composed of hot red chilies, vinegar, salt and sometimes garlic. Indonesian or Malay Sambal Oelek is an example.

Cilantro:
leaves of the coriander plant. Also known as Chinese parsley.

Coconut milk:
the liquid extracted by squeezing the grated meat of a coconut; most often found in canned and frozen forms.

D

Daikon:
a large white radish, also called icicle radish, used raw or cooked as a vegetable – and also finely grated as a condiment.

F

Fish Sauce:
A thin, brown and salty liquid made from salted anchovies. Vietnam, Thailand and the Philippines produce this condiment, where it is used much like soy sauce is used in Japan or China.

Furikake:
a condiment for rice made with shredded and seasoned dried seaweed and fish flakes.

G

Ginger:
the gnarled rhizome of a tall, flowering plant (Zingiber officinale) native to China. In Hawai'i, where it is grown, it is most frequently used fresh. Though also available powdered, pickled or candied, these forms are not good substitutes for fresh ginger.

H

Hawaiian Chili Pepper:
a very small (1/2 to 1 inch long) and extremely hot pepper, similar to the Caribbean bird chili.

Hawaiian Salt:
Coarse sea salt.

Hokkigai:
a type of clam available canned in Japanese grocery stores.

I

'Inamona:
Hawaiian word for a relish (in paste or chopped form) made from roasted kukui nuts and usually salt.

J

Japanese Cucumber:
smaller and thinner skinned than most cucumbers, this can be substituted with the youngest American cucumbers available, peeled and seeded.

Julienne:
To cut a food into thin strips similar in size to matchsticks.

K

Kim Chee:
a very spicy Korean vegetable pickle – usually Chinese cabbage. The main seasonings are red chilies, garlic, ginger and green onions.

Kim Chee Base:
the pickling brine for kim chee pickles. Available bottled at Asian markets.

Kukui Nuts:
> the Hawaiian name for the nuts of the candlenut tree; a main component of 'INAMONA.

L

Limu:
> Hawaiian word for all types of plants living in the water or damp places. The use of the word limu today generally applies to only edible seaweeds. Edible seaweeds can be purchased at seafood stores and Hawaiian delicatessens.

Limu Kohu:
> a highly prized edible red seaweed that may range in color from tan through shades of pink to dark red (Asparagopsis taxiformis).

Limu Lipoa:
> and edible brown seaweed genrally sold in a preserved salted form. (Dictyopteris plagioramma or Dictyopteris australis)

Limu Manauea:
> See OGO.

Lomi:
> Hawaiian term meaning to massage or knead.

Lū'au Leaf:
> young taro leaves that must be cooked thoroughly 50-60 minutes before eating. Spinach makes an acceptable substitute.

M

Macadamia nuts:
> rich, slightly sweet nuts that are a major crop in Hawai'i; often called "Mac Nuts".

Mango:
> a sweet and aromatic fruit that ranges in size from 1/4 to 2 pounds and tastes like a slightly resinous peach. Varieties range in color from greenish yellow to red when ripe.

Maui Onion:
> large white onion noted for its sweet flavor, grown in Kula, the up-country region of Maui. Substitute with other sweet onions, such as Vidalia.

N

Nori:
> dark green, purple or black sheets of dried seaweed with a slightly briny flavor. Sheets are paper-thin and may be either plain or flavored with soy sauce, sugar and sometimes chili pepper. The flavored type of nori is called AJITSUKE NORI.

O

Ogo:
also limu manauea, the type of seaweed most commonly referred to in Hawaii simply as "limu". Color can range from green to reddish brown; its filaments have a crisp texture and a mild flavor. (Gracilaria coronopifolia and Gracilaria bursapastoris)

Opihi:
edible limpet that is highly prized, and is a luau staple. This small, abalone-like shellfish is eaten raw.

Oyster Sauce:
a concentrated dark-brown sauce made from oysters, salt and soy sauce. Used in many Asian dishes to impart a full, rich flavor.

P

Pepeiao Akua:
Hawaiian word for a tree fungus also known as Jew's ear.

Poke:
Hawaiian word meaning to slice or to cut into small bite-size pieces; refers to a traditional Hawaiian dish of raw seafood, fresh seaweed, Hawaiian salt and Hawaiian red chili peppers.

Pupu:
Hawaiian word meaning appetizer or snack to go with drinks.

R

Rice Paper:
thin, translucent sheets made of rice used in Vietnamese cooking as a wrapper. These can be found at Southeast Asian markets.

Rice Vinegar:
a type of vinegar made from rice wine; generally clear with a pale straw color. Generally, rice vinegar is mellow and lower in acid than other vinegars.

S

Sambal Oelek:
see CHILI PASTE.

Sashimi:
Japanese dish of the freshest fish served raw. Sashimi-grade fish is the highest quality fresh fish for the purpose of eating raw.

Sesame Oil:
oil pressed from the sesame seed is available in two forms. Pressing the raw seed produces and oil, which is light in color and flavor and can be used for a wide variety of purposes. When the oil is pressed from toasted sesame seeds, it is dark in color with a much stronger flavor. It is this darker version that is to be used in the recipes of this book.

Sesame seeds:
the edible seeds of a plant of the Pedaliaceae family that have a

distinctive nutty flavor. They come in black or white varieties, and are known as benne seeds and goma.

Shichimi Togarashi:
A Japanese seven spice mixture that contains ground chili peppers, black pepper, dried orange peel, sesame seeds, poppy seeds, hemp seeds and dried nori seaweed. Available at Japanese grocery stores and Hawaii supermarkets.

Soy Sauce:
a sauce made from fermented boiled soybeans and roasted wheat or barley; its color ranges from light or dark brown and its flavor is generally rich and salty. Used extensively in Chinese and Japanese cuisines as a flavoring, condiment and a cooking medium.

T

Tako:
Japanese name for octopus.

Taro:
Tahitian word for a starchy tuber that can be baked or boiled like potatoes or pounded into a paste called poi. The large green taro leaves can be eaten, but must be cooked thoroughly to remove oxalic acid crystals, which cause a prickly sensation in the throat. Cooked spinach can be substituted for cooked taro leaf.

Teriyaki:
Japanese cooking technique that uses a soy based sauce for meat or fish.

Tobiko:
Flying fish roe. The tiny orange-colored fish eggs – smaller than salmon caviar – are used for sushi and other dishes.

Tofu:
Japanese name for a bland soy bean curd that can be custard-like in texture or quite firm. The firm or extra firm varieties are generally used in stir-frying or deep-frying.

W

White Crab:
a pale grey crab with subtle spots sold at Hawaii fish markets and is often served raw. The carapace is 3 to 4 inches wide.

Wok:
a round or flat-bottomed Chinese cooking pan used for stir-frying or deep-frying foods.

Z

Zest:
the colored portion of a citrus fruit's rind. When removing the zest from a citrus fruit, it's important to avoid removing the bitter white pith just below the colored portion.

FISH SHOPPING TIPS

If buying the fish whole (this is often the case with aku), look for bright colors and clean appearance. Eyes should be clear and bright with black irises. Skin should be unbroken, and if the fish has visible scales, the scales should be intact and firmly attached. (There is one exception to this rule: if fish has been gaffed, there will be a gash on the head. This is acceptable.) When touched, the abdomen should be firm and elastic.

If buying the fish in blocks, look for bright, clear color without brown or green shades. Avoid stringy white gristle and blood spots. The odor should be fresh and clean, not "fishy." Most supermarkets will have a sticker with a "buy by" date on it. Choose the block according to the above criteria, then check among your final choices for the latest "buy by" date.

Buying fish at a fish market will often give you a better choice of fish, and in general, will offer fresher fish as well. If you are going to consume the fish raw, it's advisable to buy the fish at a store that specializes in seafood. This said, it's still possible to buy bad fish at a fish market, just as it's possible to buy good fish at a supermarket. Your efforts in using the criteria to select high-quality fish are ultimately more important than where you buy the fish.

Honolulu Seafood Markets

The following are seafood stores recommended for buying fish:

O'ahu Market, corner of North King and Kekaulike Streets
This group of stalls sells some of the freshest fish you'll find in Honolulu for the best prices. Many of the fish are

sold whole, and the fishmongers are all willing to scale and gut the fish for you. Some stalls specialize in larger fish that are cut in blocks for sale, and here you will find premium cuts of 'ahi for sashimi. Be sure to ask for what you want.

Tamashiro Market, 802 North King Street
This fish market is the favorite of many Honolulu residents, and offers a good selection of 'ahi grades and cuts. Tamashiro's staff is famous for their knowledge and good service, and will give good cooking advice. Edible seaweeds are also available here.

Ward Farmer's Market, 1020 Auahi Street
This group of stores will provide nearly all the specialty ingredients called for in this book. They include:

Haili's Hawaiian Foods
This stall is one of the few places where you can buy 'inamona and various types of edible seaweed along with fresh 'ahi and other seafoods.

Marukai Wholesale Mart
Although this store requires that you become a member for a fee, the fee is reasonable enough to justify your joining, even if you may not shop at this store often. The wonderful selection of specialty Japanese ingredients made membership a good thing indeed. Nori, premium quality rice, excellent cuts of 'ahi and other seafood, a wide selection of miso and other condiments and fresh shiso leaves can all be bought here.